National Parks

By Sharon Fear

CELEBRATION PRESS
Pearson Learning Group

The following people from **Pearson Learning Group**
have contributed to the development of this product:

Joan Mazzeo, Lisa Arcuri **Design** | **Editorial** Betsy Niles, Linette Mathewson
Christine Fleming **Marketing** | **Publishing Operations** Jennifer Van Der Heide
Production Laura Benford-Sullivan
Content Area Consultant Dr. Linda Greenow

The following people from **DK** have
contributed to the development of this product:

Art Director Rachael Foster

Carole Oliver, Ross George **Design** | **Managing Editor** Scarlett O'Hara
Helen McFarland **Picture Research** | **Editorial** Kate Pearce, Amanda Rayner
Ed Merritt **Cartographer** | **Production** Rosalind Holmes
Richard Czapnik, Andy Smith **Cover Design** | **DTP** David McDonald
Consultant David Green

Dorling Kindersley would like to thank: Johnny Pau for additional cover design work.

Picture Credits: Corbis: 24tl, 30b; W. Perry Conway 16tl; Pat O'Hara 7tr; Galen Rowell 13b; Patrick Ward 17b. Gerald Cubitt: 27cl. Eye Ubiquitous: Derek Cattani 29b. FLPA – Images of nature: Tom and Pam Gardner 5br; Tony Hamblin 15tr; Minden Pictures 26–27; Mark Newman 12tl; Silvestris 10bc; Larry West 30tr. Getty Images: Gavin Hellier 9br. Robert Harding Picture Library: Geoff Renner 10–11. Lonely Planet Images: Trevor Creighton 25br. National Geographic Image Collection: Bill Hatcher 8br. Nature Picture Library: Ingo Arndt 5cr; Nigel Bean 1; John Cancalosi 8tl; David Curl 24cl; Jeff Foott 4br; William Osborn 25tr; Anup Shah 28b; Jeremy Walker 6–7. N.H.P.A: 18–19, 19tr, 21tr, 21b; Andy Rouse 28cr. Pictures Colour Library: Picture Finders 13tr. Woodfall Wild Images: 14–15. Jacket: ImageState/Pictor: front t. Vireo: W. Peckover front bl.

All other images: DK Dorling Kindersley © 2005. For further information see www.dkimages.com

ISBN: 0-7652-5228-7

Color reproduction by Colourscan, Singapore
Printed in the United States of America
2 3 4 5 6 7 8 9 10   08 07 06 05 04

1-800-321-3106
www.pearsonlearning.com

Coyote Ridge Elementary School
13770 Broadlands Drive
Broomfield, CO 80020
720-872-5780

Contents

What Are National Parks?

Our world is a beautiful and interesting place. Mountaintops rise up to the clouds. Canyons give us glimpses deep into the ground. Lakes and rivers glint in the sun. The world is also home to millions of **species** of plants and animals. National parks all over the world help preserve many of these wonderful landforms and species.

☐ Grand Canyon National Park, United States

A national park is an area protected by a nation's government. Mining, farming, building, and hunting are usually banned in national parks. Most national parks protect animals, plants, and natural landscapes. Some protect historic places. A few parks protect the culture, or way of life, of the **native** peoples who live in them.

☐ Kruger National Park, South Africa

Creation of National Parks

The United States created the world's first national park, Yellowstone National Park, in 1872. Yellowstone has 10,000 hot springs and 200 **geysers** like this one. Today, there are more than 4,000 national parks around the world.

☐ Glacier National Park, Canada

☐ Lake District National Park, England

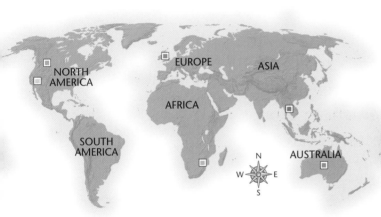

☐ Khao Yai National Park, Thailand

The national parks covered in this book are from six separate regions of the world. They are very different from one another. Each has its own unique plants, animals, and landforms. Yet all of the parks share two common goals. One is to protect the land and the plants, animals, and people who live in the parks. The other is to educate people about the natural wonders found in these parks.

☐ Uluru-Kata Tjuta National Park, Australia

Grand Canyon National Park, United States

At Grand Canyon National Park you can see 2 billion years of Earth's history carved in rock. The park is located in northwest Arizona, in the United States. The scale of this rocky landscape is breathtaking.

Apart from the unique landforms, the canyon and its rims, or borders, are also important historically. They were once home to several Native American groups. The U.S. government decided such a special place should be preserved.

United States
Arizona

Name: Grand Canyon National Park
Location: Arizona, United States
Established: 1919
Area: 1,904 square miles
Visitors per year: 5 million

The Landscape

The Grand Canyon is one of the world's deepest canyons. It was carved out by the Colorado River. Imagine a huge gash in the Earth, measuring 6,000 feet at its deepest point and 15 miles at its widest point. The steep, red canyon walls are more than one mile deep. Each layer of rock shows a different period in Earth's history. The bottom layers existed long before dinosaurs lived on Earth.

The walls of the Grand Canyon are made up of approximately forty different rock layers.

How the Canyon Formed

The canyon is a **plateau** that was slowly raised up. Wind and rain slowly wore it down. Then the rushing waters of the Colorado River began carving out the canyon 6 million years ago. The river still carries away hundreds of thousands of tons of rock, gravel, and sand every year.

Mexican spotted owl

Hunting, feeding, or approaching wildlife in the park is against the law.

gray fox

Wildlife

The park spans many different **elevations**, so it has several **habitats**. Hundreds of animal species live in these habitats. Many of these species are rare, native, and **endangered**.

Near the river, coyotes, skunks, tree frogs, and rattlesnakes are common. In the inner canyon, thousands of bats and several endangered California condors roam the desert skies. In the forests, more than fifty mammal species can be found, including porcupines, black bears, foxes, and elk. Lizards and owls also live in the forests.

porcupine

People and the Park

The park is important to the history of native peoples. Native Americans have lived here for thousands of years. Today, about 600 Havasupai (HAV-uh-soo-pay) are the only native people in the area. They live in the remote inner canyon. Park visitors can visit the Havasupai village and museum.

The park also provides lodging and several activities for visitors. Hiking, rafting, and biking are some ways people explore the canyon. Sightseeing tours are also popular.

The park's popularity means more pollution and **erosion**. Park rangers make sure that visitors follow the rules so that the Grand Canyon will be there for future generations to enjoy.

Some adventurous visitors ride mules to the bottom of the canyon.

The Havasu Falls, located near a Havasupai village, are a popular spot for picnics.

Glacier National Park, Canada

Imagine a park full of ice and snow. Jagged, snow-capped mountain peaks tower over valleys. Rivers and waterfalls rush throughout the park. Avalanches crash down the hillsides. This is Glacier National Park in British Columbia, Canada, where an icy wilderness forms one of the world's natural treasures. No one has ever settled in this icy, rugged place.

British Columbia

Canada

Name: Glacier National Park
Location: British Columbia, Canada
Established: 1886
Area: 521 square miles
Visitors per year: 600,000

Avalanche
An avalanche is a fast-moving, tumbling flow of rock, snow, and ice. Changes in temperature or vibrations from loud noises or small earthquakes can cause avalanches.

The Landscape

The park is best known for its 400 glaciers. Over time, these slow-moving rivers of ice helped carve out the rugged and varying **terrain** of the park. The park has many different climates and habitats due to the changes in elevation. High up on the mountains is the **alpine tundra**, which is too cold even for trees to grow. A temperate rain forest lies in the valleys, one of just a few cool and damp rain forests in the world.

Many trails within the park offer spectacular views of the glaciers.

Glaciers Change the Land

Glaciers form when snow falls in places where it's too cold to melt. As the snow builds up over many years, it turns to ice. When the buildup of ice becomes heavy, it begins to move slowly downhill, carrying boulders and gravel as it goes. The rock grinding against rock causes erosion. Thousands of years ago, this kind of erosion created the park's deep valleys.

Cutaway of a Glacier

moving ice

direction of flow

Moose are strong swimmers and can cross lakes many miles wide.

Grizzly bears hibernate for half the year, so they look for enough food to last for six months.

Mountain goats' hooves are well adapted for rocky surfaces.

Wildlife

Glacier National Park is home to many large animals, including deer, moose, and elk. Black bears and grizzly bears search for berries in the valleys. Mountain goats climb along high, rocky mountain ledges.

Mountain caribou also live in the park. They are an endangered species. Caribou migrate to find food in winter. They need a lot of space in which to live. In other places, people are pushing the caribou off the land. In Glacier National Park, no one interferes with their natural habitat.

People and the Park

The special challenge for this park is keeping visitors safe. Park rangers look for signs of avalanches. They also provide up-to-date information about the weather conditions.

Still, the danger doesn't keep visitors away. Tourists come to hike, mountain-climb, camp, and ski. As well as the thousands of people who visit the park every year, another 3.5 million drive through on the highway. The managers of the park limit human activities to keep this precious landscape safe.

The Railway

The transcontinental railway was built about the same time the park was founded. It linked Canada from east to west and ran through the park. The railway owners hoped the snow-capped scenery would attract tourists. The Canadian government allowed the railway owners to build one hotel, and it's still the only hotel in the park.

Mountain climbing is a popular sport at Glacier National Park.

Lake District National Park, England

Farms and wild spaces sit side by side in Lake District National Park, in northwest England. Low mountains are ringed with green valleys and lakes. The mountains, meadows, woods, and valleys are dotted with villages and farms.

The British government wants to keep this land as unspoiled as possible. However, the Lake District is different from most other national parks because many people live and work there. About 42,000 people live in the national park. They are, however, outnumbered by 730,000 sheep.

United Kingdom

England

Name: Lake District National Park
Location: northwest England
Established: 1951
Area: 885 square miles
Visitors per year: 12 million

The Landscape

Lake District National Park is the largest of England's eight national parks. It is the site of England's highest mountain and largest lake. The park's central mountains are steep and jagged. Rounded, lower hills surround them. Long ago, glaciers scooped out hundreds of lakes in the area.

There are strict rules about how park land can be used. Builders need permission to build. People must have licenses to fish in lakes and streams. Farmers are only allowed to use a few chemicals for farming.

Scafell Pike is England's highest mountain.

The varied landscape of Lake District National Park attracts many visitors.

England's largest lake is Lake Windermere.

Wildlife

The park's habitats include mountains, wooded valleys, pastures, lakes, and **moors**. Each habitat supports different kinds of wildlife. Mountain cliffs are nesting sites for the peregrine (PEHR-uh-grihn) falcon. Lake shores attract many birds. The vendace fish is an endangered species that lives in these lakes. Another rare species, the natterjack toad, lives here, too.

More peregrines live in the Lake District than anywhere else in Europe.

Otters can be found in many of the rivers within the park.

The natterjack toad blends into its surroundings so it's difficult to see.

People and the Park

The Lake District National Park area has thousands of years of human history. Stone Age people hunted and farmed there 5,000 years ago. Then the ancient Romans built roads and villages there. The people who live in the district now are careful to preserve its historical sites.

Visitors hike, bird-watch, swim, or just enjoy the scenery. The park's popularity helps many of the residents who run hotels and restaurants and sell goods to tourists. Students and scientists come to study the unique wildlife. The park service also offers many courses and lectures each year.

Kayaking is popular in the Lake District.

Hikers take a moment to enjoy the landscape at Lake District National Park.

Kruger National Park, South Africa

Stretching for 220 miles along northeastern South Africa, Kruger National Park is the country's largest national park. Elephants, zebras, lions, and giraffes all roam freely on the park's grassy plains. Nature lovers visit this wildlife reserve to admire hundreds of species of plants and animals. There, even the rarest species are safe from harm sometimes caused by humans.

Zebras roam in herds on the plains of Kruger National Park.

AFRICA

South Africa ☐

Name: Kruger National Park
Location: northeast South Africa
Established: 1898
Area: 7,580 square miles
Visitors per year: 500,000

The Landscape

The park is mostly flat, with some low hills. It lies in a **savanna** region, which has grassy plains with a few trees, dense bush, and shrubs. The area has a wet and a dry season. In the dry season, when rainfall is very low, not many plants grow. There is, however, enough rain in the wet season to sustain shrubs and trees. Some **subtropical** forest grows along the banks of the park's rivers.

Plant Life

Plants are specially adapted to their savanna habitat. They have developed many ways to protect themselves. Many shrubs and trees, such as the acacia, have long thorns to protect them against grazing animals. The large trunk of the baobab tree, shown above, stores moisture for times of drought.

Wildlife

The park's savanna and forest provide homes for many kinds of wildlife. Savanna grasses, shrubs, and trees support huge herds of herbivores, or plant-eating animals. Giraffes, elephants, impala, warthogs, and hippopotamuses all survive on plants. Carnivores, or meat-eating animals, such as lions and leopards, hunt on the plains. Several hundred species of birds also live in the park, including many hornbills. Zebras, buffaloes, and baboons live on the plains, and crocodiles are common in the rivers. There are also around 250 endangered black rhinoceroses.

Giraffes can reach up high to eat the leaves on tall trees.

People and the Park

The park offers many activities for visitors. People can explore by walking one of the wilderness trails with an experienced guide. They may also drive on more than 1,500 miles of roads.

It is important to protect the park against damage because many endangered species live there. Visitors may travel only between sunrise and sunset, unless they are on a guided night safari. After dark, people must leave the park area or stay in one of the fenced-in rest camps. This protects both the animals and the people. In addition, park rangers carry out important **conservation** work. Thanks to their hard work, the wildlife continues to thrive.

Visitors to the park can stay in special fenced-in rest camps.

A group of tourists watch wildlife from a safe distance.

Uluru-Kata Tjuta National Park, Australia

What's the biggest rock in the world? It's 1,100-foot Uluru (oo-lah-ROO), the giant red rock located in the Uluru-Kata Tjuta (KAH-tah JOO-tah) National Park. The park is located in central Australia. Aside from Uluru and the Kata Tjuta rocks, the landscape is mostly flat, sandy plains.

Uluru is recognized by nearly everyone in Australia. It has become a symbol of the heart of the country. At sunset, visitors watch it take on spectacular colors in the changing light.

Name: Uluru-Kata Tjuta National Park
Location: Northern Territory, Australia
Established: 1958
Area: 485 square miles
Visitors per year: 650,000

Uluru, shown here, is an Aboriginal name meaning "great pebble."

At sunset, the domes of Kata Tjuta glow many colors. They change from pink and orange to red and purple.

The Landscape

Uluru and Kata Tjuta, a group of large sandstone rocks, are the highlights of the park. Uluru is not only the world's biggest rock, but it is also one of the world's oldest. Millions of years ago, it was once an island in a lake. Kata Tjuta is a group of stones with rounded tops. About thirty of them are scattered around the park. Like Uluru, they stand high above the flat plain.

Uluru-Kata Tjuta History

These lands traditionally belonged to the first people of Australia, the Aboriginal people. In 1985, the government returned the land to the Anangu Aboriginal people. Uluru-Kata Tjuta is the Aboriginal name for this place. Now the Anangu people, some members shown below, and the Australian government manage the land together.

The thorny devil lizard stays cool by absorbing moisture through its skin.

Wildlife

The animals that live in this desert habitat have to survive very hot and dry conditions. Native mammals include kangaroos, dingos, bats, and various small marsupials and rodents. Many species of birds, such as parrots and thornbills, can also be found. Reptiles, including thorny devil lizards and woma pythons, are well suited to this habitat. Foxes, cats, rabbits, and other species, introduced into Australia in the past few hundred years, compete with native animals for food.

Wallabies survive the hot climate by resting under trees.

At the base of Uluru, a natural flow of water sustains the animals and plant life.

People and the Park

Uluru-Kata Tjuta is a sacred place to the Aboriginal people. The rocks and the trails nearby play important roles in their history and their stories. Visitors are asked not to climb the rocks. The Anangu people want the park to remain unspoiled. They are the caretakers of the region and wish to protect the land.

Visitors to the park can hike or drive around the rocks or tour the park on a camel. They can also learn a great deal about the Anangu. Park rangers give educational talks every day about the lives and traditions of the Aboriginal people.

Aboriginal art appears in rock caves at the park.

Although not native to Australia, camels are used to take people around the desert landscape.

Khao Yai National Park, Thailand

Khao Yai National Park in northeast Thailand includes many different habitats—rain forests, grasslands, and mountains. Perhaps the most fascinating are the steamy forests filled with exotic flowers, birds, and animals. It is the amazing variety of living things that makes Khao Yai so special.

Today, forest covers only about a quarter of Thailand as rain forests are being destroyed for wood and farmland. Khao Yai was the first national park to be established in Thailand, and its continued protection is important.

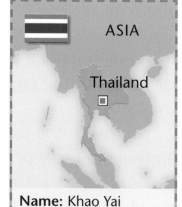

ASIA

Thailand

Name: Khao Yai National Park
Location: northeast Thailand
Established: 1962
Area: 770 square miles
Visitors per year: 1.4 million

Visitors to Khao Yai can enjoy hiking or bird-watching in the park's forests.

The Landscape

Within the park there are several mountains that stand more than 3,000 feet tall. The park is the source of five important rivers that nourish the land. There are also many beautiful waterfalls.

The grasslands contain many plant species, while evergreen and **deciduous** trees grow in thick forests. Tropical rain forests are the most interesting feature of the park. Rain forests like these are remarkable because they are home to more than half of all the plant and animal species on Earth.

Haeo Suwat (HAY-oh soo-waht) Waterfall is one of many waterfalls found in the park.

Layers of a Rain Forest

Most plants and animals live in the canopy layer because it receives the most sun and rain. The forest floor is home to large animals that hunt on the ground, and plants that grow in damp areas, such as ferns.

emergent layer - - - - -

canopy - - -

understory - - - - - - - -

forest floor - - - - - -

Wildlife

Thailand's tigers, elephants, and gibbons are all endangered. These animals are protected from harm by humans within Khao Yai National Park. Other large animals found in the park include monkeys, leopards, bears, deer, and wild boars.

Most of the park's wildlife inhabits the rain forest areas, which are also home to many species of insects, bats, tree frogs, and snakes. There are more than 300 species of birds, including the Siamese fireback pheasant—Thailand's national bird.

Saturn butterflies are protected in the park.

There are only around 500 tigers left in Thailand.

White-handed gibbons live in the tropical rain forest.

People and the Park

Visitors can explore the park in many ways. People are encouraged to hire a guide to lead them on the various hiking trails. They can also access special viewing towers for a look at rare animals. Park rangers also organize night drives for visitors to look for creatures that are active at night.

To better protect wildlife, no hotels or tourist facilities have been built in the park. Sometimes, however, visitors are given permission to stay overnight in small houses within the park. If humans take care, Khao Yai will continue to be a safe home for hundreds of species of plants and animals.

Visitors take an elephant ride with their guide through the park's forests.

The Future of National Parks

As the world's population grows, more and more land is being used for housing and farming. Animals and plants are losing their homes and food supplies. As a result, many species are in danger of becoming **extinct**. The establishment of national parks is one way in which some of the Earth's natural habitats, landforms, plants, and animals are being preserved.

This signpost warns of potential dangers and instructs park visitors how to behave.

Visitors enjoy the amazing view at Grand Canyon National Park.

Glossary

alpine tundra a type of habitat that is above the tree line on mountains

conservation the care and protection of forests, water, and other natural resources

deciduous shedding leaves yearly

elevations heights above sea level

endangered in danger of dying off

erosion the wearing away of rock or soil by natural processes, such as wind, water, and ice

extinct condition in which all the plants or animals in a species have died

geysers springs that shoot boiling water and steam up into the air

habitats kinds of places where a plant or animal lives

moors open stretches of land with few trees; often swampy

native belonging to a place

plateau a large, flat area that is raised above the surrounding land

savanna a flat, open region with few trees

species a group of closely related living things

subtropical a warm climate; nearly tropical

terrain land and its natural features

Index